be
kind.

A Radically Different
Approach to Leadership

be
kind.

GUI COSTIN

Founder **dakota**

WITH

MORGAN HOLYCROSS

LIONCREST
PUBLISHING

BE KIND
A Radically Different Approach to Leadership

FIRST EDITION

ISBN   978-1-5445-4966-8 *Hardcover*
        978-1-5445-4965-1 *Paperback*
        978-1-5445-4967-5 *Ebook*

To all leaders who make the bold leap to lead with kindness,
knowing that the words they choose can transform people's lives.

Contents

Introduction

It's easy to be a dick.

It's easy to give yourself permission to say whatever comes to mind, regardless of how it makes the other person feel.

But is that the best way to lead?

In the past, companies were defined by their physical capital—their buildings, equipment, and machinery. In the modern environment, however, companies are defined by their people—the individuals who have the institutional knowledge of how to get a job done. The most successful organizations learn how to keep their best people, hopefully forever.

As a leader, you play a big role in determining whether people stay or walk out the door with their institutional knowledge. Employees generally leave bosses, not companies. That means the way you treat people, the words you use, what you say, and how you say it—these all influence individuals' decision to stay or go. If people can tell you don't really care about how you treat them, they will leave.

Maybe you've never thought about the impact your words have on your team. Consider this: Have you experienced a lot of turnover? Does morale seem low? Do you wonder why people aren't responding to your direction? There's a good chance your words and treatment have something to do with those kinds of employee disengagement.

Maybe you have thought about how your words land, but you think that if you soften your approach, people will take advantage of you. Or maybe you're convinced that people won't be as productive if you don't come down hard on them, and the quality of your product or service will suffer. Traditional leadership styles often include intimidation, toughness, and micromanagement as the best way to get results.

I believe there's a different way, one that involves vulnerability on your part—but not at the expense of results. I believe it's possible to lead with kindness *and* create a hard-charging culture. It's possible to have fun while striving for excellence and playing at the highest level. It's possible to treat people with thoughtfulness without lowering expectations or avoiding accountability.

It's possible to have your cake and eat it too.

MY JOURNEY TO HARD-CHARGING KINDNESS

I believe this hard-charging-but-kind leadership approach is possible and worth pursuing because I've seen it in action.

My journey began as a business entrepreneur. In 1998, I

joined a startup as the lone salesman. In 2006, my partner and I launched Dakota, a sales and marketing company for investment firms. The first five years were incredibly stressful and volatile—typical startup challenges, difficulties getting established, and partner conflicts that led to a split in late 2009. I pressed on, and with the help of my longtime assistant, Tracy, I started hiring salespeople.

Then in 2011, I had an epiphany: Life is extremely empty when focused solely on oneself. This realization marked the beginning of a new leadership journey for me and a new direction for Dakota as a whole. We developed a mission statement and put it on our website: "Help other people get what they want out of life." This guiding principle eventually became formalized as The Dakota Way—time-tested principles for becoming a world-class fundraiser by focusing on what matters most (the subject of my last book). It also became my personal mission, something I still follow today.

Up until that point in 2011, my leadership style could be characterized as forceful, confrontational, and flippant, like the stereotypical football coach. I gave myself permission to say whatever I wanted, regardless of how it made someone feel. I never got into the demeaning or judgmental zone, but there were a lot of "snaps" when I became frustrated.

With a small team of male salespeople, that locker room approach worked. The guys all tolerated my overly direct, sometimes mocking tone when they didn't meet expectations: "Are you kidding me? I told you this ten times already!" (And, yes, there were usually a few cuss words mixed in.)

Then we hit our first major growth phase and our sales

team expanded. As we diversified, I realized my approach needed to change. I wasn't perfect—in moments of frustration, I still occasionally erupted into "Gui-canoes" and spoke more harshly than I should have—but I did start softening my tone and paid more attention to the words I used.

The final refinement came with hiring my friends' daughters in 2020. Now I had accountability. Even if they never reported back to their parents, I acted as if they might—as if whatever I did might appear on the front page of tomorrow's newspaper.

In addition, I recognized that my locker room approach had never truly served anyone's best interests. Snapping in moments of frustration can have far-reaching negative impacts—on the individual, the work culture, and the success of the organization. We really are playing with fire when our leadership style is more volatile and less compassionate.

After hiring my friends' daughters, I suddenly saw so clearly that I could no longer erupt as I had in the past. I could no longer give myself permission to say whatever came to mind, no matter how frustrated I felt. That didn't mean lowering my standards. I simply recognized once and for all that I needed to approach every conversation with kindness and consideration.

How did my shift toward kindness impact Dakota's success? Within the next five years, we grew from twelve to ninety employees and increased our revenue to $30 million. Focusing on kindness didn't decrease productivity and success. It greatly improved both. It also made the workplace more stable—volatility dropped, trust increased, and the team genuinely had more fun.

People enjoy working at Dakota. They know what's expected of them and they deliver. By placing the right people in positions to execute with tools to succeed, and treating them with respect and kindness while maintaining clear expectations and discipline, we have been able to achieve remarkable results as a team.

LEADERSHIP ISN'T ABOUT THE TITLE OR THE BADGE. IT'S ABOUT THE IMPRINT YOU LEAVE ON THE PEOPLE WHO CHOOSE TO FOLLOW YOU.

A RADICALLY DIFFERENT APPROACH

This book isn't a how-to manual on running a business. It's not a playbook for scaling (though you can scale faster with happy teammates), and it certainly isn't filled with corporate jargon or formulas. I'm not here to tell you how you should or shouldn't lead your company. What I *am* here to do is share what I've learned about keeping your most valuable people while driving a hard-charging culture that still knows how to have fun.

This book presents lessons learned about leading through kindness. In the chapters that follow, we'll discuss:

- The difference between being nice and being kind
- The importance of vulnerability and being comfortable in your own skin as a leader
- The role of trust in creating a healthy culture

- How leaders can reduce volatility by establishing and upholding core principles and clear expectations
- The importance of fun in building a cohesive culture and propelling the team toward high achievement
- The lasting impact your words can have on those you lead

Everyone brings their childhood experiences into the workplace—how they were raised and the lessons they internalized. These formative experiences inevitably surface when someone assumes a leadership position. Without clear guidance, new leaders often fall back on inherited wisdom: "My father told me if I'm nice, people will walk all over me. No one will respect me."

I'm inviting you to rethink the leadership lessons you may have learned along the way. I'm also challenging you to self-reflect on your own words and the impact they have on those you lead.

I'm not suggesting that you become a timid and complacent leader. People need strong, confident direction. They require clear expectations, effective communication, and a compelling vision. At the same time, they need leaders who trust them, who have their back and remove obstacles so they can get the job done.

They need leaders who treat them with hard-charging kindness.

1

Start with the End in Mind

Who was your favorite high school teacher and why?

This is one of my favorite leadership questions because no matter who I ask or where the person went to school, the answer is nearly always the same: "Mr. Art Teacher or Ms. Science Teacher because he/she treated me like a friend."

My favorite was Mr. Berg, my high school English teacher. He understood me and supported me. He let me be me, without judgment. That didn't mean he let me skate by in class. Every time I turned in a paper, it came back looking like a sea of red. For two years, I never got higher than a C in his class. Mr. Berg had tough conversations about my performance, but he never demeaned me or made me feel stupid. He treated me like a friend.

Fast-forward twenty-four years when I was coaching high school golf at a private school with a coat-and-tie dress code. I was standing at the first tee, along with a group of students still in their uniforms and a few teachers who came to watch the match.

Suddenly, I heard a teacher call out to one of the students, "Hey, Smith, nice tie." I looked back and saw Smith, whose tie was a little lopsided.

All these years later, that incident has stuck with me. The teacher could have walked up to the student and said something like, "Joe, you're too good looking to have your tie hanging down here. Let me help you straighten it a bit." Instead, he chose to demean the boy in front of his friends.

This teacher was not a bad person. He just took the "it's easy to be a dick" approach. He gave himself permission to say the first thing that came into his head without considering the impact on the student. He chose the easy way—sarcasm over care. And that choice left a lasting scar. If this moment still lingers with me after all these years, I can only imagine how deeply it must have stayed with Smith.

Too many leaders follow the example of the second teacher. They give themselves permission to be sarcastic, disrespectful, and even mean. While students don't usually have the freedom to walk away if they're treated like that, employees do.

If your people are your greatest asset, then your only real job is to create a culture so good employees would be crazy to leave. At Dakota, that is exactly my goal. And not through fear or manipulation, but by creating an environment that's so engaging, so supportive, and so fulfilling that leaving means going to a worse culture. In this chapter, we'll talk about what that kind of workplace looks like.

A CULTURE PEOPLE DON'T WANT TO LEAVE IS
THE ONLY TRUE COMPETITIVE ADVANTAGE.

WHAT DOES UTOPIA LOOK LIKE?

The data is clear: People leave companies because they don't like how they're being treated. According to the Great Attrition study by McKinsey, "not feeling valued by their manager" was one of the top three reasons employees quit.[1] Another study found that employees who feel excluded are 39 percent more likely to quit (actual turnover).[2]

The cost of replacing this institutional knowledge is enormous. When you have people who know how to get the job done and require little oversight, you've struck gold. Any organization—whether it's a tech company or an apartment building with a doorman—benefits tremendously when people deeply understand their roles.

As leaders, then, we all need to ask ourselves what kind of environment we need to create to get people to stay. What does utopia look like?

I believe utopia is a culture of kindness. It's an environment where everyone is treated with respect and like

1   Bonnie Dowling et al., "The Brave New (Business) World," *People & Organization Blog,* McKinsey and Co., February 7, 2022, https://www.mckinsey.com/capabilities/people-and-organizational-performance/our-insights/the-organization-blog/the-brave-new-business-world (accessed September 15, 2025).

2   BetterUp Labs, "The Connection Crisis: Why Community Matters in the New World of Work," BetterUp Labs Report, 2022, https://globewomen.org/globaldiversity/wp-content/uploads/2023/03/BetterUp_-The-Connection-Crisis-Colloquium-on-Global-Diversity.pdf (accessed September 17, 2025).

responsible adults who don't need to be micromanaged. Where they are not teased or made fun of. In this kind of culture, people can be the best versions of themselves and truly thrive. They feel empowered to be productive and get things done. People derive an enormous amount of gratification at finishing projects. At the same time, they become frustrated when they feel prevented from doing so. Unfortunately, many leaders create an environment where projects get started but not finished. They don't provide the resources to help their people complete their work.

Utopia is also a culture in which people are given clear direction *and* the autonomy to accomplish their work in the way that makes the most sense. The most successful businesses move faster as they grow. What often happens as companies grow, however, is that bureaucracy creeps in, layers of decision-makers are added, and decisions take much longer to make—if they are made at all. Employees feel frustrated because they can't get answers or approvals that would enable them to get the job done most efficiently. A good leader removes those obstacles—whether they're people, situations, or resources—so the team can complete their projects and enjoy that rewarding sense of accomplishment.

Some leaders fear kindness means lowering standards. The truth? It raises them. At Dakota, high expectations and kindness fuel each other—and the results prove it. We treat people with kindness and respect. We create an atmosphere of camaraderie and fun. At the same time, we have high expectations. I don't have the time or energy to be a babysitter. Individuals either fulfill their roles and do their jobs, or they move on. When people realize this, and see that they have the freedom to do their job in the way that makes the most sense, they step up. They play at the highest level.

BEING NICE VERSUS BEING KIND

I'll tell you one thing utopia is not: It doesn't mean being nice. Many leaders miss the important distinction between being *nice* and being *kind*.

In a nice culture, leaders focus on creating a "Kumbaya, we're all going to get along" atmosphere. That means they avoid difficult conversations. They see where people are messing up but they don't want to hurt anyone's feelings, so they don't address issues head-on. They ignore the fact that someone keeps taking advantage of their work-from-home privileges. They let it slide when the top salesperson is repeatedly rude to someone in the office.

These leaders might rationalize their decision by saying something like "I don't want to ruffle any feathers" or "I don't want to step on their toes." I think they're actually making excuses for why they didn't address the issue. They were trying to be nice, thinking this is the same thing as being kind.

It's not. Avoiding tough conversations might be the nice thing to do, but it's not kind—it's actually unkind. Not addressing issues is bad for the individuals involved, because they don't grow and improve, and it's bad for the organization as a whole.

Years back we had a young employee I'll call "Priscilla," who worked on our film studio sales team. We had a situation where I needed to ask Priscilla a direct question about an action she had taken. Unfortunately, Priscilla's answer was incongruent with what another salesperson said. To get to the bottom of this "he said, she said" situation, I looked through Priscilla's email and discovered she had twisted the truth when she answered my question.

At that point, I took twenty-four hours to process the situation, but I knew what needed to happen. I needed to stand up for Dakota's core principles. Lying violated our "Do the right thing" policy, so Priscilla had to go.

If I cared about being nice, I might have talked to Priscilla but not fired her, or maybe I wouldn't have talked to her at all. I like Priscilla. She is an outstanding salesperson. But she had violated one of our core values. Keeping her wouldn't have been kind to Priscilla, since she wasn't a cultural fit for Dakota, and it wouldn't have been kind to the rest of the sales team who did uphold these important core values.

When you lay out your principles so transparently like we do at Dakota and somebody violates them, you have all eyes on you wondering, "Coach, you said all this stuff about your core principles. Now what are you going to do? Are you going to take action, or are you going to roll over because they're the number one person?"

Letting Priscilla go was definitely one of the hardest things I've ever done, but it was also the kindest thing I could do for her and for the company.

LEADING BY EXAMPLE

Creating a culture of kindness is really about how you as the leader treat people. It's about the words that come out of your mouth. You can be kind and deliver difficult messages at the same time. You can confront tough issues in a way that builds people up and even makes them feel good, rather than destroying them.

When I talked to Priscilla, I said, "Look, you really messed up. You've lost the trust of the team. That doesn't make you a bad person. But I can't stand for one thing and then tolerate something else. As a young leader who is going to be very successful, you have to live by your words."

Today, Priscilla is killing it in her current job, and we have a great relationship. However, things probably would have turned out differently if I would have lost my temper with her. I may have thought things like *I can't believe you lied! What were you thinking?* but I didn't give myself permission to say them.

Unfortunately, many people in leadership positions can't help themselves. They say the first thing that comes to mind. Or their words always carry a hint of undermining or teasing. For example, if they call a team member and the person is out on the golf course, they might say, "Must be nice! I'm here working away." That kind of guilt-tripping serves no purpose except to make the person feel bad about taking time off. Instead, why not say, "Nice! Hit 'em well. We can talk later."

Leaders frequently justify comments like this because they think they're being funny or that harsh words are motivational. They may have grown up with this style of feedback. But these passive-aggressive interactions tear at the fabric of culture and relationships. They imply judgment about how others use their time and undermine kindness in the workplace.

Judgment is one of the most corrosive elements in any organization. People do not perform at their best when they feel judged and labeled. Let's say one of your employees has a reputation for partying hard on Friday nights. What's the best way to effect change? Not by labeling him "The Party Guy" or "The Friday Night Guy." That comes across as mocking and judgmental. Instead, see the guy as a human being and talk to him about approaching weekends more thoughtfully: "These are your best years. I get it. Have a blast! But try to stay fresh and healthy, too, so you're ready to kill it on Monday morning."

Likewise, there's a kind alternative to passive-aggressive comments. When an employee is watching the game at his desk, you can ask, "What's the score?" When someone is leaving for the gym, you can say, "Enjoy the workout—I'll see you when you get back." Taking this approach requires confidence. You have to be secure enough to let people make their own schedule, manage their own time, and use different working styles. (We'll talk more about this kind of confidence in Chapter 2.)

Of course, if there's an actual performance issue—if someone is consistently missing deadlines or neglecting responsibilities—that's a different conversation. Have that discussion at another time, and address the issue head-on.

As a leader, you set the tone. In your day-to-day interactions with team members, as well as when you're addressing tough issues, be cordial and respectful. Talk to people the way you would speak with friends (minus the mocking if that's part of your close relationships). Your team will start to treat everyone else the same way.

Also, don't underestimate the power of acknowledgment. My friend "Kevin" runs a sixty-person sales organization and has an impossible-to-please boss. The way Kevin treats his teammates and allocates human resources makes him a world-class CEO. Yet he receives no recognition for his exceptional performance. That lack of acknowledgment is incredibly discouraging, even as a successful CEO.

Everyone wants to know their hard work and efforts are seen. Unfortunately, taking time to recognize teammates is uncommon, which makes it powerful when someone actually does it. Be that kind of leader. You never know what a compliment or shout-out will mean to the recipient. They may have worked incredibly hard to improve themselves and deeply appreciate the recognition.

REQUIRES INTENTION

Everything I've discussed points to one critical idea: Creating a culture of kindness requires intention. It doesn't happen by accident. You need to thoughtfully construct an environment where communication flows freely, decisions are made efficiently, obstacles are removed, and people feel trusted and respected.

I believe that starts with setting clear standards for behavior. At Dakota, our number one standard is to treat everyone with kindness—it's our No A-hole policy. You don't hear anyone making fun of anyone else, teasing them about something they said or a mistake they made, calling somebody out publicly, or making jokes at someone's expense. That just doesn't happen.

I also believe that creating a kind environment means embracing first principles thinking as a leader: the ability to strip away preconceptions and get to the fundamental truth of a situation so you remove obstacles and allow your people to get their work done. When making decisions, ask, "What is the best outcome for this situation? What is the best way to go about doing this if no one's ego were involved?" Too often, decision-making gets bogged down in opinions and hypotheticals rather than focusing on the clearest path forward.

I've watched our team work through prioritizing technology updates. We had one major update that required significant work but wasn't the highest priority. Rather than debating endlessly, we simply decided, "That's the biggest lift but not the most urgent. Let's put it at the end of our queue, after these smaller, higher-priority items."

When you make decisions this way, you can feel the weight lift off everyone's shoulders. Enabling people to work on what matters most and what can be accomplished quickly shows kindness to your team members and adds value to customers.

Remember: Your people are human so they will say stupid things and make mistakes sometimes. It happens. How do you respond when it does? Do you correct them publicly? When you do that no one feels good—not the person being corrected or anyone listening. At that point you've lost the room as a leader. You've violated the No A-hole policy. Sometimes choosing not to comment is an act of kindness.

When you intentionally establish a culture with clear principles around communication, autonomy, and treating people like adults, there's lower volatility in the tone of the business. People aren't walking around on eggshells. They can relax and do their best work.

PAUSE BEFORE YOU SPEAK. CHOOSE KINDNESS OVER SARCASM, CLARITY OVER AVOIDANCE, AND BUILD A CULTURE SO GOOD YOUR PEOPLE WOULD BE CRAZY TO LEAVE.

LEADERSHIP WORTH ASPIRING TO

Mr. Berg was my favorite teacher because I didn't feel judged by him. He had high standards and clear expectations, but he also let me be me.

Kids love their grandparents for the same reason: They don't feel like they're being judged or micromanaged like they do at home. With their parents, kids can feel like they hear constant criticism: "Clean your room." "You left your dishes in the sink." "Why didn't you take out the trash?" With their grandparents, they feel loved and accepted, like I did with Mr. Berg.

As a leader, be like Mr. Berg. Be like a grandparent. Give your people a culture of kindness where they can thrive.

Establish clear principles and expectations, remove obstacles, and treat everyone with respect. Let them make their own decisions about how to get their work done without fear of judgment and ridicule.

In this type of culture, kindness becomes the through-line that connects everything else—the high expectations, direct conversations, lack of micromanaging, and low volatility. People find it extremely hard to leave this kind of fun, engaging, productive environment.

Leadership is not about what title you hold or how much power you wield, but how intentionally you create the conditions for others to thrive. That's the kind of leadership worth aspiring to.

So, if creating a culture of kindness encourages employees to stay and perform at the highest level, why don't all leaders do it? That's what we'll discuss in Chapter 2.

KINDNESS CALL TO ACTION

1. *Don't give yourself permission to blurt out the first thing that comes to mind.* Pause, consider the impact, and choose words that build up rather than tear down.
2. *Build a culture so good people don't want to leave.* Not through fear or perks, but through kindness, clarity, and respect.
3. *Stop confusing "nice" with "kind."* "Nice" avoids the tough conversations. "Kind" has the courage to hold people accountable with respect.

2

Vulnerability

When you walk into the offices of an investment firm that will remain nameless, you'll notice one signature feature: video cameras in every single office and conference room. Every conversation is recorded, every day, 365 days a year. Every conversation is viewed and critiqued, and employees are regularly subjected to a verbal dressing-down as a result.

The co-chief investment officer claims these cameras provide "radical transparency." I call it creepy. That camera policy takes micromanaging to a whole new level.

Contrast that leadership style with Reed Hastings, the co-founder of Netflix. No camera in conference rooms or offices. No traditional performance reviews. Netflix doesn't even have a travel and entertainment policy. Employees are trusted to spend what they need to spend to do their job.

Reed doesn't have lower expectations than the other company's co-CIO. He challenges people to play at the highest level. But he also trusts his employees to act like adults, and he's willing to take the chance that some might take advantage of him. So far, Reed's vulnerability has paid off and has created an atmosphere where people are allowed to be the best versions of themselves and excel at what they do.

In this chapter we'll show how vulnerability is actually a strength as a leader and the key to creating a culture of kindness.

> LETTING GO OF CONTROL ISN'T
> WEAKNESS—IT'S THE GREATEST ACT OF
> KINDNESS A LEADER CAN SHOW.

THE VULNERABILITY MYTH

One of the biggest myths in leadership is that if you're kind, people will take advantage of you. This fear holds many leaders back. They believe that kindness signals weakness, that giving people autonomy means they won't work hard, and that trust will be abused. As a result, they micromanage, lead like dictators, and treat people like children.

The real issue is vulnerability, or lack thereof. Many leaders aren't comfortable enough in their own skin to let their people operate without micromanagement. They can't sit with the perception that people may view them as weak and take advantage of them. They're often obsessed with controlling everything their team does because they're focused on themselves and their reputation, speaking of work projects as "my this" and "my that." With that mindset, it's not surprising they micromanage their people. They need to make sure they look good.

Being vulnerable means you have to trust people. You have to trust the skilled, responsible adults you hired to get the job done.

This kind of vulnerability is a lot easier and simpler when you have extreme clarity on what you stand for. When everyone understands the standards and operating principles, they are less likely to violate them. At Dakota, we don't have a PTO (paid time off) policy—I don't even know how that works. Team members can take time off whenever they want. People often ask, "How can you operate without a vacation policy?" That question reveals the fear we're talking about: They assume employees will take advantage of the situation.

At Dakota, people don't abuse the policy. They know I'm not there to babysit. They know that if they want to be treated like adults, they need to act like adults—even if they're only twenty-two and straight out of college. They're expected to play at the highest level like everyone else, and they know they can look for work elsewhere if they don't. With those expectations in place, I have no fear of being taken advantage of.

When I'm traveling, I'm not stressing about what everyone is doing every day I'm gone. Are they working a full day? Are they meeting deadlines and calling clients? I don't keep track. They know our principles and what's expected of them. I'm trusting they're doing their job.

I'll make a distinction here: I make phone calls all the time to ask the team questions. I try to provide guidance because we work in a business where I have deep domain expertise in the industry, as well as databases and user interfaces. I can simplify and short-cut a lot of processes. That's not micromanaging; that's being a resource to help the team get their jobs done.

ROOTS IN UPBRINGING

In many ways, the ability to be vulnerable and comfortable in your own skin comes down to upbringing. Everybody's parented in a certain way. If your father taught you that the world is out to get you and you should never let somebody have the upper hand on you, then as a leader, you're less likely to show vulnerability.

My dad was highly volatile. He teased me and constantly put me down. As a result, early in my career, I showed up as an angry, competitive micromanager. I wasn't vulnerable. Over the years, I have worked hard to change that mentality.

Teachers and coaches can also impact your willingness to be vulnerable. Many teachers and coaches communicate with demeaning comments, put-downs, and teasing in order to control fourteen- to eighteen-year-old kids. In that environment, you grow up with a beat-down mentality through middle school, high school, and college—a sense that you have to protect yourself so you're not taken advantage of. When you become a leader, your natural response is often to repeat how you have been treated.

The coach of a successful Division 1 team is a perfect example of what *not* to do. Coach "Johnson" has been there for twenty years, teaching each group of players that it's "us against the world." He encourages his team to talk smack to opponents during warmups and call the opposing coaches names. It's the most corrosive form of leadership I've ever seen—and unless taught differently, those players will carry it into the workplace.

WHO AM I TO JUDGE?

We talked about judgment in Chapter 1 and how corrosive it can be to your organization's culture. When you judge someone, you're basically insulting them. You're setting yourself up on some pedestal and looking down on the other person and whatever they did.

As a leader, you need to be self-aware. When you see your own mistakes, you'll have an attitude of "Who am I to judge?" when someone else messes up. You'll have real compassion, because you've been there. This is a sign of vulnerability.

I have adopted this attitude with my kids, as well as my employees. I know I've screwed up more than they ever will. So who am I to judge? That doesn't mean I avoid conversations when they screw up, but it does mean I approach them from a place of understanding.

If you clearly establish what good looks like, then when someone makes a mistake, you can talk to them as a compassionate coach. Don't publicly call them out or label their work as poor. People need to know it's okay to get something wrong. Help them see the mistake and understand what to do differently next time.

As a leader, you want confident employees. Why? They

perform better, quicker, and continuously look for ways to improve. According to one study, 97 percent of confident employees seek ways to improve their work, as opposed to 87 percent of their less confident teammates.[3] The best way to build confident employees is to let them make decisions. Let them make mistakes without being ridiculed or shamed. Let them learn, pivot, and keep going.

To let that happen, you as a leader have to be vulnerable.

As the CEO, I don't call each salesperson daily, weekly, or even monthly and ask, "What are your goals? What are you doing to get there?" As a company, we're clear about our values and goals. Our salespeople know the direction we're heading in, and they're the ones charting the course.

I don't review expense reports because trust is the kindest policy. Micromanaging signals distrust. Freedom signals belief. If somebody's truly going off the reservation, I'll find out sooner or later and then I can reel them in, but otherwise, I let it go. That's not the best use of my time, nor do I want to create a bureaucracy to manage a travel and expense policy.

You may not deal with expense reports, but there are probably other tasks you don't need to micromanage. Figure out the best use of your time, the things you can (and should) control, and let the rest go. You have better things to do that can help your teammates and your customers.

By not micromanaging every action and decision like

---

3   U.S. Merit Systems Protection Board Office of Policy and Evaluation, "Confidence in Ability to Perform Successfully," research brief, September 2021, https://www.mspb.gov/studies/researchbriefs/Confidence_in_Ability_to_Perform_Successfully_1868023.pdf (accessed May 27, 2025).

a crazy controlling person, you allow everyone to operate with a lower anxiety level. Sure, you'll experience moments of higher anxiety, but overall, the whole atmosphere will be calmer. Fear hinders performance and leads to unnecessary mistakes, and in an already fast-paced environment, we want our team to perform to the best of their abilities.

STANDARDS AND PRINCIPLES

One of the most talked about but still underestimated, underutilized, and underappreciated concepts in business is documenting what you stand for and why. Establishing standards and core values is also a key way to help yourself be vulnerable: If the team knows what's expected, you can step back and let people live by those standards.

Here are a few guidelines for determining your principles:

Standards should be built organically. Every company has its own DNA and its own unique ideas on what matters most and what "good" looks like. The company standards should naturally flow out of these values. They should feel like an organic fit with the organization as a whole, not a copy-paste from another company's website.

These standards should also have room to grow as your team continues to grow. They shouldn't be stagnant. At Dakota, our standards have developed over time, since I founded the company in 2006, and they will keep growing as our team continues to grow.

Standards and core principles need to be in your company's vernacular. If you build standards organically, their wording will naturally fit your company. At Dakota, we captured our core principles using short, fun, easy-to-remember phrases, for example, "Walk the eight feet." "Don't go cowboy." "We sell apples to apple buyers; we don't try to convince orange buyers to buy apples." "We're not in the convincing business." "Throw your hat over the wall." "Focus on what you can control."

You will most likely never hear another company use these phrases; they probably don't even know what half of them mean. But everyone at Dakota knows "Walk the eight feet" means "Don't guess how to respond to a customer email or guess how to build a report in Salesforce. Walk to your teammate's office (eight feet away), and talk to them." They know "Throw your hat over the wall" means committing to something even if you don't feel fully ready: Put a deadline and figure it out.

Once you establish your standards, have fun naming them in a way everyone will remember.

Your standards should inform decision-making. Whenever the need for a decision comes up, everyone should be able to ask themselves, "Is this consistent with our standards or not?" For example, at Dakota, we stand for responsiveness. Why? Because it's the right way to be. The customer is important. Teammates are important. We value being respectful and responsive when people reach out and ask for help handling a situation. So if someone takes six hours to return an email, that's not consistent with our principle of responsiveness and a standard five-minute response time. The person knows they should have made a different decision.

Once you establish your standards, you can share them

with any new teammate on their first day of work. You can say something like, "These are what we stand for. This is how we treat people. This is how we make decisions. This is not tolerated." Related to creating a culture of kindness, at Dakota we tell people right up front: We have a No A-hole policy—we don't belittle or put people down. We don't have little inside jokes or tolerate passive-aggressive behavior. We're just going to get our job done and be good teammates. And we're also going to have a ton of fun at work.

Having these core values in place makes it much easier for you to be vulnerable and take the chance that people might take advantage. People know what's expected, and they know there will be consequences if they behave badly or don't follow the company standards. At that point, you simply need to have a tough conversation. No passive-aggressive comments. Be kind and tell them the truth: It doesn't seem like they're a good cultural fit, and it might be best to part ways.

DEFINE YOUR PRINCIPLES, SET HIGH
STANDARDS, AND BE VULNERABLE ENOUGH
TO TRUST YOUR PEOPLE TO LIVE BY THEM.

THE BIGGEST RISK

Many leaders think being vulnerable is a big risk. I think the bigger risk is *not* being vulnerable. If you're a jerk and treat people poorly, you give them all sorts of reasons to exhibit bad behavior. However, if you treat people with kindness, set clear expectations, and remove all the excuses for not being able to get their job done, they have no choice but to excel and play at the highest level—or leave. There are no more fingers to point, no more excuses.

When team members know the boss has their back and has their best interests at heart, they step up. Why would they be irresponsible with vacation time or the company card if this person trusts them and takes care of them?

Being treated like an adult, being allowed to make mistakes, learn, and grow—these all communicate trust on the part of the leader. As you'll see in the next chapter, being trusted is a top priority for employees, and vulnerability opens the door to building that trust.

KINDNESS CALL TO ACTION

1. *Set high standards.* Kindness doesn't mean lowering the bar—it means expecting the best from your people.
2. *Create your own principles.* Define standards unique to your culture so everyone knows what "good" looks like.
3. *Be vulnerable enough to trust.* Let go of control and give people the freedom to rise to the expectations you've set.

3

Trust

My friend "Jay" used to be the CEO at one of the largest asset management firms in the world. In the early years, he'd negotiate with other companies, make a decision, get approval, and move forward. He knew exactly what to do and was trusted to do it.

As the company grew, however, things changed. Bureaucracy creeped in. He couldn't simply negotiate a deal. Instead, every decision had to go through four layers of approval.

It finally became too much. The fun factor of the job was gone because he wasn't being treated like an adult. Jay was no longer trusted to make a decision without micromanagement, even though he had been CEO for thirteen years. So he left.

This is the perfect example of what can happen if you don't create a culture of kindness in which team members are trusted to get the job done. Yes, I'm saying it's unkind to layer in bureaucracy where there are simply too many people involved in decisions. The result is that you lose your best people, and the institutional knowledge goes out the door with them, which over time is death to an organization.

Trust is perhaps the most underutilized and underappreciated concept in leadership. When your team trusts you, and when they know you trust them, they will perform at higher levels. It's a two-way street that forms the foundation of any successful organization.

> TRUST SCALES. BUREAUCRACY
> DOESN'T. CHOOSE TRUST.

WHAT COMMUNICATES TRUST

How do employees know that the leader trusts them? They see it in words and actions.

THE WORDS YOU USE MATTERS

First and foremost, trust is built through the words you use to interact with your team. We all know that person who makes flippant comments to tease, demean, put down, and embarrass others. If you're that person as a leader, you'll massively erode the trust factor. You have to learn to control what comes out of your mouth. You may *think* of a "funny" or sarcastic comment, but you don't have to say it.

Leaders who give themselves permission to poke fun or ridicule are like teachers who mock students to keep them in line. It's a kind of beat down that establishes them as the person in charge. That's absolutely a way to lead, but not a good one.

ASK FOR INPUT

To create a culture built on trust, you can't always be the person with the answer. You need to show that you value other people's opinions. If someone comes to you for a decision, for example, first ask, "What are your thoughts on this? What do you think we should do?" Then follow up with additional questions to unpack their thinking. Make people feel seen and heard.

Asking someone's opinion face-to-face is also important in building trust because there's no hiding behind a screen or a phone. There's no option for silence and waiting. Face-to-face conversations make it easier to get to the heart of a decision. We see this all the time on our sales calls: People are more engaged, see the value more clearly, and are more likely to ask meaningful questions.

GIVE YOUR OKAY

Another way to communicate trust is to give your okay on projects, even if they're not 100 percent perfect. Doing so keeps things moving and implies that you trust the person's judgment so far and you trust them to finish the final pieces.

That doesn't mean sacrificing quality; you still need to trust but verify. However, if projects are repeatedly delayed because you're not giving your okay to something that truly is okay, your team will wonder if you think they are incapable of making a decision or completing a project.

If you want to drive people out of your company, that kind of distrust is the fastest way to do it—outside of treating them poorly. My stance is: Do everything you can to encourage people to move faster. Their desire is often there, but they need to know you're removing obstacles to help them work at speed.

MANAGE BY THE RULE, NOT THE EXCEPTION

Too many leaders manage by the exception, not the rule: In other words, they create policies based on the actions of a few and everyone gets penalized.

Think of small-town councils, piling rule on rule after one minor incident. Soon the bureaucracy chokes the work itself, and the town has a long list of policies—about skateboards on sidewalks or not being allowed to play a ball game in parks—that really aren't necessary because they apply to so few citizens. Rule after rule after rule. That kind of bureaucracy wears people down.

The same happens in business. There's an incident—for example, someone posts something slightly off-brand on social media or an employee takes a slightly longer lunch break—and management creates a whole new process around that one thing that hardly ever happens, for example, only the Chief Marketing Officer can only approve posts or the whole company has to clock in and out of lunch. Not only does this make for longer processes, but people aren't able to focus on their tasks at hand, which hinders productivity. That's how you get bureaucracy—you put rules on top of rules on top of rules.

Instead, focus on creating fewer policies that have a big impact. On your most critical, must-do tasks, have tight constraints. Beyond that, treat people like adults and address the exception as what it is: an exception.

LET PEOPLE MAKE DECISIONS

Yes, I've already said this, but letting people make decisions is one of the most important ways to let your team know you view them as trusted responsible adults.

My co-author, Morgan, is now in charge of the Dakota blogs. She comes up with the topics, runs them by me, and then writes the articles. Sometimes I'll send her ideas and then she'll write the posts in the way that makes sense to her. In either case, I let Morgan decide how to write the post and then check in to verify the direction matches my vision. If it doesn't, I let her decide how to incorporate my feedback.

People value being given direction *and* the space to figure out how to get there using their own decision-making. The latter communicates you have faith in them.

THE IMPORTANCE OF TRUST

In an article titled "The Neuroscience of Trust," Paul Zak found that people who feel trusted at their companies also report the following benefits:[4]

- 74 percent less stress
- 106 percent more energy at work
- 50 percent higher productivity
- 50 percent planned to stay with their employer over the next year
- 13 percent fewer sick days
- 76 percent more engagement
- 29 percent more satisfaction with their lives
- 40 percent less burnout

Isn't this what you want at your firm? Creating an environment that fosters less stressed, less burned out, more energized, more motivated teammates leads to keeping your best people.

I've seen this time and time again at Dakota where individuals are able to get stuff done simply because they know we have full trust in them. I only need to give the greenlight or come back with edits. Putting this trust into my team allows them to have full reign.

---

4   Paul J. Zak, "The Neuroscience of Trust," *Harvard Business Review*, January–February 2017, https://hbr.org/2017/01/the-neuroscience-of-trust (accessed May 27, 2025).

WHAT ERODES TRUST

We've already discussed one action that erodes trust: putting up roadblocks and impeding your team's ability to make decisions and get work done. People derive great satisfaction from starting and completing projects. When you're slow in giving an answer or require multiple approvals, you prevent that from happening, in addition to communicating lack of trust.

A second factor is how you react to ideas offered by your people. Let's say someone proposes a fix to a current problem or a suggestion for streamlining a process, but it's really not a good idea. How do you respond?

If you react with something like "Come on. Really?!" or "That'll never work!" or "What are you thinking?" you have eroded trust with that employee and anyone else within earshot. The person making the suggestion will likely second-guess themselves, and everyone who heard you will probably think twice before they make a suggestion themselves. Why would they if they don't feel confident in themselves or your trust in them? As a result, you and the company could miss out on valuable ideas.

Instead, try to understand where the person's coming from. Say something like "Walk me through your thinking. I think I hear you, but I'm a little confused on why we would do this. I might be totally missing something." Once they explain, you could say, "Okay, I see what you're trying to do. That's not a bad idea. Is there another way to go about it? Let's think that through."

Even if an idea is wildly off-base, blunt honesty beats ridicule. Kill the idea, not the confidence. If you're in a group, say something like "Hey, I hear you. Let's take this offline." Then afterward, walk them through your thinking: "Look, I totally see where you're coming from, but I think going in that direction would have X, Y, Z effects that wouldn't be positive."

In both cases, you're enrolling the person in rethinking their idea, without criticizing or demeaning them. And perhaps most importantly for building trust, the person feels heard.

There's a third way to erode trust: having a middle management layer. Think about it: What is middle management's job? Most of the time, they're in charge of making sure people are getting their job done—that shows a complete lack of trust. Many companies are eradicating this layer for this very reason. Facebook, for example, recently fired all their middle managers because they realized everybody needs to be a player-coach. They don't need anybody in between. Whether they realize it or not, nearly every other organization could do the same.

At Dakota, we have a fifteen-person inside sales team, but we don't have an inside sales manager. That position would be a waste of time since the account executives who work with the inside salespeople can play that leadership role. An inside sales manager simply adds a layer of bureaucracy and slows people down, which erodes trust, as we've said. Why waste everyone's time like that?

WHAT TRUST DOESN'T MEAN

So, does trust mean you should let people do whatever they want? No. We're talking about a balance between letting people make decisions, take initiative, and complete projects on their own while checking in to make sure they're on the right path.

Here are two key ideas around what trust doesn't mean.

GOING COWBOY

At Dakota, one of our core principles is "Don't go cowboy." In other words, don't go off and do your own thing without communicating. Going cowboy would be like Morgan writing an article about pink unicorns and posting it to the Dakota blog without talking to anyone about it. We all need to tap into the wisdom and feedback of others. Chances are what someone has completed isn't perfect—and if it is, that person is one of the few wizards out there. Tapping into the collective knowledge of an organization is of the utmost importance.

The overall genius of the best organizations is how they communicate. There's a culture of sharing what people have learned, what's working and not working, where they're stuck. That last piece is super important. As a leader, you need to create a safe environment, one where people can ask for help without worrying about being ridiculed or put down.

At Dakota we have twelve meetings a year to ensure we have this kind of ongoing open communication. We call them W Days and their sole purpose is to find out what's working, what's not working, and how we can help. W Days aren't meetings—they're trust in action. When people know they have regularly scheduled opportunities to speak up and even complain, they are less likely to go cowboy. That rhythm is the trust in action.

GIVING UP DECISION-MAKING ENTIRELY

About ten years ago, I was talking with a friend who owns several businesses and said, "Your CEOs kind of run with their own strategy at each of the different companies, don't they?"

"No way," he replied.

"Why not?"

"Gui, if those guys drive the truck into the ground, they can quit and go get another job and get a salary. I have to then take over. I own that company, and I have to get it out of the ditch."

His response communicates this point clearly: As a leader, you're not showing lack of trust in any way, shape, or form when you make the *big* decisions. Those decisions should be made collectively with a team, but you as the leader eventually have the final call. That's your job.

Jeff Bezos once said there are two types of decisions: two-way doors and one-way doors. You can come back from a two-way decision if it's not working: For example, if you schedule meetings on Mondays and then remember a lot of federal holidays fall on Monday, you can pick another day. One-way is just that: You make that decision and you cannot come back. Shutting down a division and laying off the team, for example, is a more permanent decision, once that is much harder to recover from. Big, one-way decisions like this cannot be delegated.

Even in those one-way situations, you show trust because you don't exist within a vacuum. You ask your leaders and teammates for ideas and help, because you trust them. You thank them along the way for the information they provide because you know it enables you to make a sound decision.

You also earn trust by explaining why you're making a certain decision and how it benefits the team. If they understand why, they may not agree, but they'll probably see how you have their back. And that goes a long way in earning trust.

TRUST STARTS AT THE TOP. CHOOSE WORDS
AND ACTIONS THAT BUILD CONFIDENCE,
EMPOWER DECISIONS, AND CREATE A
CULTURE WHERE PEOPLE THRIVE.

TRUST STARTS AT THE TOP

Like the culture of kindness as a whole, trust starts with you. As a leader, you need to be self-aware and self-disciplined: aware of how your words and actions communicate trust, or lack thereof, and disciplined in controlling what comes out of your mouth. You don't have to say everything you think. It's like waiting twenty-four hours before you send an angry email: Learn to pause, even for ten seconds, before you make a comment that could erode trust in an instant.

Creating an environment in which people feel trusted is like teaching a man to fish rather than handing him a fish. If you teach him how, he can feed himself forever. Likewise, if you treat people as adults and let them make decisions, they become much more independent and self-reliant, and they can complete projects far more efficiently and effectively. When people feel trusted, when they feel like their boss has their back and is removing barriers to help them get work done, they can show up as the best versions of themselves and perform at the highest level.

In that kind of environment, you have happy, engaged people who enjoy coming to work. Does that mean the office is conflict-free? No, but when you've built this culture of trust, conflict becomes an opportunity for growth, as we'll explore next.

KINDNESS CALL TO ACTION

1. *Use your words wisely.* Sarcasm, ridicule, and flippant comments erode trust faster than anything else. Speak with clarity and respect.
2. *Empower people to decide.* Give direction, then trust your team to make decisions and learn without going cowboy.
3. *Don't punish the many for a few*. Avoid creating endless rules for rare exceptions. Trust people to act like adults.

4

Conflict

"Jordan" had been with the company from the beginning. For years, he was our only sales person and he took pride in that role. But as the company grew, we hired more salespeople so Jordan had to share the spotlight. He did not like that and became increasingly irritable and difficult to work with.

Finally, I sat down with him. I suspected what was going on, but I asked questions so he could tell me in his own words.

"Jordan, what's going on? I feel like you've been off the past few months," I said.

"I just don't feel like things are the same," Jordan replied.

"What do you mean by that?"

"I don't know my lane anymore."

Finally I said, "Look, are you bummed out that we're adding salespeople?"

At that point, Jordan melted down. "I just feel like I helped build this place, and now I'm being pushed out. I don't even know where I fit anymore. I feel lost."

I nodded. "Well, you know you have to make a decision, right? Are you going to get with the program that we are growing or are you going to move on?"

At that point in my career, I had learned a key lesson: As leaders, you sometimes act like therapists. In the face of conflict, therapists don't lose their temper. They don't rush to judge. When present behavior is inconsistent with past behavior, that often means something's cooking, and it's the boss's job to understand what's really going on. That requires compassion.

Conflict is unavoidable, but how you handle it is completely within your control. When you build a foundation of trust, conflict becomes an opportunity rather than a threat, a chance to build and enhance relationships rather than hurt them. It's also an opportunity to train and educate your team on what "good" looks like, which is one of the leaders' most important roles.

CONFLICT ISN'T THE ENEMY OF
CULTURE—UNKINDNESS IS.

WHAT GOOD LOOKS LIKE

It's your job to define what good looks like, whether that's responding to customer emails within minutes, or matching your company's sleek branding when creating sales documents, or arriving at the office at 7:15 a.m. for the 7:45 a.m. check-in. When someone isn't meeting those standards, it's also your job to address that fact head-on. You have to be uncompromising about showing everyone what good looks like.

Expecting people to perform at the highest level naturally leads to conflict, because you're asking them to get out of their comfort zone on a continual basis. But that conflict doesn't have to involve an argument or hurtful comments. You can address thorny, uncomfortable issues from a place of support.

For instance, if Morgan sends me a well-written blog post that still needs a few things cleaned up before we can send it out, I don't insult her. I might say, "Hey, that's not how we would describe our data. We need to adjust that to say X, Y, Z."

My comment doesn't mean Morgan did a bad job; the blog simply isn't 100 percent the way I want it to read. If we're playing to win and serving the customer—which is what we've agreed to as a company—then details matter. In this case, "good" is explaining our data in a specific way.

Before we hired our data wizard, Khizar, I helped our data team go through a complete mental reset. I had to redefine what good looks like when it comes to inputting data. In the past when someone was asked, "Can you enter these hundred contacts into the database?" the answer was usually some version of "Yes, but I'll have to stop what you asked me to do last week, so that's going to slow things down."

That's not a recipe for scaling a data business. That response comes from a scarcity mentality, and I realized that needed to change.

In a conversation with "Hank," one member of our data

team, I said, "We have to think in the law of abundance. If I ask you to get a million contacts in, the answer is going to be, 'You got it. We'll get it done. We're going to come back to you with a timeline.' You're not going to tell me something else is going to suffer. We're going to have elasticity in our team to handle any project we need."

I also threw myself under the bus and said, "I have to reset myself too. It has to start with me."

Not ten minutes later, we were discussing another data set, and Hank said, "Yeah, we can do that, but—"

"Hank, what happened to ten minutes ago? What happened to abundance?"

He laughed and said, "Yeah, okay, it's going to take a while."

"That mindset ended ten minutes ago," I replied. "For the rest of our lives, we're only going to think in abundance, and we're going to be able to get anything done in a timely manner."

As a leader, you have to be uncompromising about what good looks like—for everyone, yourself included. Yes, it will lead to conflict sometimes, but you can move through those conversations with kindness.

HANDLING CONFLICT WITH KINDNESS AND COMPASSION

To make sure conflict becomes an opportunity for relationship *building* and not *breaking*, you need to find a balance: Make your point strong enough so people know you're serious while remaining calm and kind. For example, I'll often smile and use humor: "Guys, am I missing something here? This product label has 'Dakota' in a different font. When did we change our logo?" With a lighthearted comment like this, I've communicated the standard without yelling or accusing someone of making the same stupid mistake for the fifth time.

People need to know you're serious about standards, but you can do that without slipping into sarcasm or contempt. This is the challenge. As a leader, you will often be far ahead of your team in terms of thinking about the direction and trajectory of the business. This doesn't mean others are performing poorly or missing the mark; it simply means you're seeing further ahead because that is what you do every day. When new programs or procedures are rolled out, conflict is inevitable: You've been contemplating and envisioning these changes for months, but they're all new for your team. They're likely to have a few "deer in the headlights" moments in which they freeze and protest the changes. In those times, compassion goes a long way. Give people grace as they grapple with the shifts. Understand that they may not be as comfortable with uncertainty as you are. Then bring people along through communication so they see what you're seeing.

SLOW DOWN

One of the best strategies is to slow down in the face of conflict. Rather than push for an immediate decision, first get agreement on what you're all trying to achieve. If you can distill the conflict down to the end goal, instead of arguing about what's happened, you can make progress.

For example, Dakota held its annual customer conference a while back. A month and a half before it happened, we were low on registrations so I looked into why. Turns out, someone had buried the registration link ten pages deep into our website. When I talked to the person responsible, we could have gone round and round on why they placed the link where they did and why I didn't think that was working. Instead, we focused on the end goal: to get more registrations for our conference. Once that was agreed on, we considered how to make it easier for people to hear about the event and sign up. Since we get two thousand hits a day on our home page, we decided to put the link at the top of the home page, along with pictures of the speakers. It worked. Registrations increased by 150 over the next six weeks.

In conflict situations when you're trying to solve a problem, don't be afraid to ask people directly, "Can you tell me what you think we're trying to achieve here?" This makes each person accountable and slows down the conversation. Everyone has to sit and consider their view of the bigger goal and everyone else's.

Often, when someone hears another perspective, they'll realize, "Oh, that actually makes sense. I never thought of it that way." That realization in itself often defuses conflict.

When you make the case by asking, "What are we trying to achieve?" and "Why?" you take all the odds out of the room. You bring everyone to the same side of the table and move away from personal opinions and who was right or wrong. In response to your questions, some people may want to debate and play devil's advocate, but that's not the goal here. You're problem-solving, not debating. And once everyone agrees on the end goal, you can figure out the best way to get there.

USE DATA

In the face of conflict, you can also use data to override opinions and avoid volatility. One of our team members showed me data about our "Book a Demo" process: We were only seeing a 20 percent conversion rate from clicking the button to completing the demo form. I tested the process and realized it required two steps: After clicking the "Book a Demo" link, people had to fill out a form and save it, and then a calendar popped up so they could choose a date and time.

We decided to shift to a simpler one-step system where the calendar pops up immediately and the person enters their information on the same page where they pick a date. In the next nineteen days, we had double the submissions with nearly a 40 percent conversion rate.

The data was clear: The original process was too cumbersome, with too many steps, and people didn't want to deal with that.

I spoke with our lead on the marketing team and realized we were following the process simply because it was the way we've always done it. We hadn't revisited this form in years. There was no need to point fingers at people and say someone did something wrong. We simply reevaluated and decided we needed to make this process as simple and easy on the visitor as possible.

EXPLAIN THE WHY

In every case of conflict, explaining the why behind the standard or request goes a long way—much further than getting angry and hurling insults.

About a year ago, we invited several people to speak at our annual customer conference and a team member followed up with an email request for a photo and bio. To me, this was like asking for favor and then saying, "Hey, do more work for me."

I talked to the person and explained my thinking: "If we're going to ask someone to speak at our conference and they say yes, they're normally the top dog at the company. You can't ask the CEO of a 1,500-person company to send you their picture and bio. It's not right to ask someone for a favor and then ask them to do a lot of work to fulfill your favor."

I didn't say this in a demeaning way; instead I used it as a teaching moment—an opportunity for growth that would have been lost had I said something like "Why are you doing that? Don't call him!"

At the same time, I offered support: "If someone says yes to speaking, come to me, and I'll go on their website, copy and paste the bio and photo, and send them to you. Then we can send both to the speaker to verify." That's exactly what happened—they added what they wanted and sent it back. But first, we did the heavy lifting.

Even if the other person doesn't agree with your approach, they will likely see that it makes sense and they will appreciate the way you handled the situation.

BE PROACTIVE

As we've said, a key part of your job is to remove obstacles. One of the most powerful ways to do this is by establishing core principles, values, and standards up front to help prevent conflicts in the first place.

If people know what's expected from day 1, they are less likely to make decisions that go against what you stand for. It will still happen, but you can simply refer back to what they already know, which makes the hard conversation a little less difficult.

Foreseeing the potential conflicts and coming up with standards and values so everybody knows what's expected is a great kindness to your people and solves a lot of your problems before they ever happen.

CONFLICT IS INEVITABLE, BUT YOUR RESPONSE DETERMINES THE OUTCOME. LEAD WITH CLARITY, COMPASSION, AND RESPECT AND WATCH CONFLICT BECOME A CATALYST FOR GROWTH IN PERFORMANCE AND RELATIONSHIPS.

RESPOND WITH RESPECT

Conflict is inevitable. The only question is whether it destroys trust or deepens it. People make countless decisions every single day; sometimes those choices match what good looks like, and sometimes they don't. Sometimes people "go cowboy" and do their own thing. As a result, you will have some level of disagreement.

The key is how you respond in the face of that conflict. You need to make your point strongly enough that people know you're serious about what good looks like, but not so strongly that your words come across as insults. Find a way to let people know you're watching and also there to support.

Don't waste the opportunity to build relationships and train your team by yelling or publicly criticizing. At the end of the day, every business is a people business, so you always have to ask yourself how you're treating those people—clients, customers, and employees alike. If you respond to conflict with volatility, you only end up hurting yourself. People don't want to be put down or ridiculed, and they will leave if that happens regularly.

If you respond with respect, however, you earn the trust we talked about in Chapter 3. You also create an atmosphere of levity, where people know their boss isn't out to crush their soul. You create a place where people enjoy the work and the company of one another—a place that's fun.

KINDNESS CALL TO ACTION

1. *Define what good looks like.* Clear standards turn conflict into a chance to raise performance.
2. *Slow down and seek understanding.* Ask questions, explain the why, and turn conflict into a chance to coach.
3. *Respond with respect.* Sarcasm and ridicule destroy relationships; kindness strengthens them.

5

Fun

In traditional college football programs, players spend countless hours practicing specific plays, running drills, and preparing for games. It's often brutal, long, boring work. Most football players don't play football because they enjoy practice—they play because they love the game itself.

John Gagliardi, a coach from Minnesota, recognized this fact and decided to try something different: He scrapped traditional practice. No playbooks, no tackling, no blocking sleds or dummies, no whistles. He didn't even want his players calling him Coach.

Instead, his team simply played football for ninety minutes every day. They practiced the game rather than components of it. And they had fun doing it.

The result? Gagliardi racked up 465 wins during his sixty years at Saint John's University, as well as twenty-seven conference championships, two NAIA titles, and two Division

III titles. As of this writing, he is the winningest coach in college football history.[5]

Gagliardi's approach transformed the Saint John's program and led to unprecedented success. Understandably, powerhouse programs like Alabama might consider this method too risky, but Gagliardi proved that creating an environment where players enjoy themselves leads to exceptional performance. His players were more invested, more focused, and ultimately more successful because they were having fun.

The importance of having fun with your team, whether on the field or in the office, cannot be overstated. It builds a cohesive culture and propels the whole group toward higher achievement. In this chapter, we'll explore what makes a workplace fun and how you can make it happen.

Fun isn't a perk. It's the fuel that makes people want to play at the highest level.

WHAT FUN IS NOT

To understand what makes a workplace fun, let's start by defining what fun is not.

Fun is not…

---

5 Adam Wells, "Winningest Coach in College Football History John Gagliardi Dies at 91," Bleacher Report, October 7, 2018, https://bleacherreport.com/articles/2799549-winningest-coach-in-college-football-history-john-gagliardi-dies-at-91 (accessed May 27, 2025).

- working for a boss who treats people poorly, uses demeaning language, publicly humiliates team members, or engages in passive-aggressive behavior
- constantly being told what you are doing wrong rather than hearing the leader ask, "What can I do to help?"
- having coworkers who are jerks (companies have a No A-hole policy for a reason, even if they don't call it that)
- going into an office where no one cares about the environment, where people aren't friendly, or where there's no coffee or food available
- working for a company that lacks flexibility in scheduling
- being part of a culture where people aren't responsive or don't finish projects they've started
- working with people who don't want to play at the highest professional level or maintain high standards
- being part of an organization without vision, communication, or accountability

When you look at this list, you'll notice that nearly 100 percent of these "not fun" attributes stem directly from leadership. The leader sets the tone and creates the environment that either fosters or hinders fun in the workplace.

YOUR ENERGY MATTERS

If the leader sets the tone, does that mean you should schedule game days or tell more jokes to create a fun atmosphere? No, that's not what I'm talking about.

Creating a culture of fun in the workplace boils down

to the one simple thing we've already been talking about: how you treat people. I don't mean avoiding the obvious—insults, name-calling, yelling, sarcasm, and generally acting like a jerk. I'm talking about the more subtle ways you interact with your team on a day-to-day basis.

As a leader, your energy and attitude are everything. It's similar to parenting—children can tell when Mom or Dad isn't happy, and the whole household feels it. The same is true in a workplace.

When you walk into the room, people can immediately sense your mood from your facial expressions and body language, as well as your tone of voice and words. If you always appear angry and upset, if your comments are usually negative or focused on finding fault, there is zero chance that your workplace will be fun. People will feel uncomfortable, like they're walking on eggshells and trying to avoid getting in trouble. What's worse, your team will perpetuate your negative energy, spreading more negativity and fault finding.

The opposite is also true: If you bring a positive energy, your team will feel it and mirror it. A sense of levity will permeate the space and put people in a more relaxed frame of mind.

So, the question is, how can you create a positive vibe on a daily basis? Here are a few suggestions:

- **Acknowledge every person every single day.** Make each individual feel like they're the most important person in the room, even if it's just for two seconds.
- **Treat your team like you would treat your friends** (minus the merciless teasing). When you're with friends,

you typically have relaxed body language. You smile a lot. You ask questions and communicate interest. You're warm and engaging, and you don't make every situation a teaching moment. Bring that same authentic energy to your interactions with your team.

- **Develop the ability to read the room**—to sense when people are shutting down, not speaking up, or not performing at their best. This awareness allows you to address issues before they become bigger problems and undermine the overall playful, lighthearted atmosphere.

In a recent meeting, "Evelyn" suggested doing a panel for an upcoming conference. I was pretty direct in explaining why I preferred individual interviews instead—one-on-one interviews for ten to fifteen minutes can draw out more meaningful content than panels where multiple people share limited time.

When I saw the look on Evelyn's face, I realized my directness might have come across as dismissive, so I made sure to acknowledge that her idea was good and clarified that we could achieve the same goal she was aiming for (creating marketable content) through the individual interview format. I unpacked the "why" behind my preference, rather than just shutting down her idea.

When you notice someone might be feeling dismissed or unheard, take the time to address it, either in the moment or afterward. Ask, "What are you thinking? How's it going?" This shows that you're paying attention and that you care about how your words are received.

Your job as a leader is simple: Make people feel better

when you walk into the room, not worse. That's the real job description. The energy in the room shouldn't shift to negative when you walk in. People shouldn't immediately feel like they're walking on eggshells. You should lift the energy up and make everyone feel great about themselves. If you can't do that, don't be a leader. People don't want to be around someone who makes them feel bad about themselves.

THE FUN-ACHIEVEMENT CONNECTION

Fun is a lever you pull to move people toward peak performance; it's not a distraction or even something that's nice to have. It's essential. When people enjoy the "game," whether a sport or their job, they play at their best. They're not stiff or rigid. They operate with a sense of playfulness that allows their natural abilities to shine through. Because they're not worried about being judged or ridiculed for making mistakes, they're free to focus on what matters—the work itself.

This is exactly what those football players on John Gagliardi's teams experienced. And it's exactly what I saw in my players when I coached high school golf.

Unlike football, golf is an individual sport. For most of the year, players compete alone. Then six times a year during golf season, I brought together these eight individuals to play as a team. It was very awkward. My role as coach was not to provide technical instruction but to manage emotions and foster positivity.

My approach was to stay out of the way and be cool. I never intervened unnecessarily or said stupid things that would make them uncomfortable or do the "cannot believe Coach said that" eyeroll. Instead, I let them hang out with their friends and have fun.

What's remarkable is that in nine years of coaching, I never once had to address the team about their performance. I never needed to have a "beat down" talk or tell them to get their act together. The team performed at an exceptionally high level—we went undefeated for two seasons—because they were relaxed, enjoying themselves, and could play at their best.

The same principle applies in the workplace. The more relaxed people are, the more comfortable they feel. And in that frame of mind, they take chances, lean into curiosity, try new things, and ultimately produce top-tier work. In this new world of AI, Agents, and LLMs, being curious, as simple as it sounds, is often the differentiator between advancing your career and being left behind.

FUN ISN'T A DISTRACTION. IT'S HOW YOU WIN. AS THE LEADER, YOUR ENERGY AND STANDARDS CREATE THE CULTURE WHERE PEOPLE THRIVE.

FUN IS WINNING

With all this talk of having fun, someone out there might ask, "Are you saying we're only here to have fun?"

If that's you, you misunderstand what I mean by "fun."

Ultimately, fun is winning, and "winning" means creating great products, trying new things, being curious, treating your teammates with kindness and respect, being responsive, providing service, and taking care of your customers and making their lives easier. All of which characterizes what it means to play at the highest level.

Fun isn't a distraction; it's how you win. When people are enjoying themselves, they take risks, move faster, and play at the highest level. These ideas are all inextricably linked together, and they all start with the leader. Not only in the leader's energy, actions, and words, but also in the standards and expectations the leader sets up.

When you establish clear standards, core principles, and values to guide interpersonal interactions, when you define what you stand for and communicate that effectively, you create a culture where people can thrive. Everyone can relax and play hard and not worry about being judged or ridiculed for making mistakes.

When you walk into a two-star motel or a six-star hotel, you know instantly which feels better. Culture is like the room—people can sense in seconds if your workplace is fun or fear-driven. You don't need to define fun explicitly; you just need to create the conditions where people feel valued, respected, and able to do their best work.

So, if you're serious about creating a culture of fun, start by looking in the mirror:

- What kind of energy do you bring into the office?
- How do you show up?
- Is your workplace fun? Do people feel like they're winning or like they're walking on eggshells?

- Do teammates feel they're growing in their careers?
- Does the company support career development?
- Can your people communicate with senior leadership if there's a problem?
- Does the CEO work to remove obstacles so people can get their jobs done?

These are the elements that make a workplace fun—not telling jokes or planning big events or adding a game room to the office, though those can be enjoyable too.

Creating a fun work environment isn't a nice-to-have; it's essential for high performance. When your team members feel supported, respected, and valued, when they see you removing obstacles to help them, when they feel like you really care about their well-being, they'll naturally give their best effort. And that's what leadership is ultimately about—bringing out the best in others so they can achieve things they might not have thought possible.

As we'll see in the next chapter, this approach stands in stark contrast to what often happens in some settings, where the leadership style can undermine performance rather than enhance it.

KINDNESS CALL TO ACTION

1. *Bring positive energy.* Your mood sets the tone. Make people feel better when you walk in the room, not worse.
2. *Create conditions for play.* Fun isn't about jokes or games; it's about trust, respect, and freedom to perform without fear.
3. *Connect fun with winning.* When people enjoy themselves, they take risks, move faster, and play at the highest level.

6

Little League

In my first match as a high school golf coach, I violated one of my own core principles: Don't ask stupid questions.

On the very first tee, "Chandler" lined up, went through his routine of setting his stance and taking practice swings—and then hit the ball out of bounds to the right. He had country miles of grass to the left. The only thing not to do was hit it to the right.

After I saw where the ball landed, I looked at Chandler and asked, "Why did you hit it out of bounds?"

I didn't yell at him, but asking "Why did you do that?" was almost worse. He wasn't trying to hit the ball out of bounds.

Chandler didn't respond, but the look on his face said it all: "Dude, I really thought you were different than that."

Too many people get into positions of leadership, whether as Little League coaches, newly selected team captains, or recipients of a new title, and all of a sudden a switch flips. They feel entitled to say whatever comes into their head—like they're the new sheriff in town and the badge gives them permission to be demeaning.

After that moment with Chandler, I vowed I would not be *that* guy.

This chapter uses the familiar example of Little League to illustrate the importance of our words and the lasting impact they can have on those we lead, whether they're eight years old or twenty-eight. I'm not here to judge. I'm writing from a place of compassion, having been that unkind coach and leader. But we all need to pause and think about how we treat people and the importance of creating a culture of kindness.

FOR THE LOVE OF THE GAME

If you coach children's sports—baseball, soccer, lacrosse, basketball, you name it—this chapter is for you. It's for all of you leaders, managers, and CEOs, too, but I want to especially highlight the impact your words and actions have on young minds.

Youth sports are supposed to be fun (remember our last chapter?). The goal is to introduce kids to a new game and let them learn to play in a nonthreatening, low-pressure environment. For some reason, however, many coaches turn Little League into the World Series and take all the fun out of the game. They treat each play like it's a life-or-death situation. They get in kids' faces and scream. They call their players names. They slam down their clipboards and throw their hats in frustration.

How is that appropriate for any age, let alone with kids who just want to run around and throw the ball and lick a Popsicle?

Let this chapter be a reminder of what matters most. You have one goal as a Little League coach: to make the experience fun. Don't be the reason kids leave sports or develop low self-esteem. When you coach at the youth level, you can have such a huge impact, both positive and negative. Create a culture of kindness on your team and be the reason your players carry confidence with them long after the season ends and into the rest of their lives.

IF KIDS FALL IN LOVE WITH THE
GAME, THEY'LL PLAY FOR LIFE. THE
SAME IS TRUE FOR YOUR TEAM.

THE TITLE DOESN'T GIVE PERMISSION

Remember the opening line of this book? "It's easy to be a dick." With kids, it's even easier to give yourself permission to say the first thing that comes into your head. After all, you're the adult. You're the one in charge. It's so easy to hold your authority over their heads.

But that makes no sense. As the adult, you should have some maturity and self-awareness about your behavior and the impact it has on others. Do you enjoy being yelled at? Do you enjoy being teased? Do you enjoy being put down in front of your friends? Probably not. So why do you treat your players (or anyone else) that way?

In any youth sports environment, the goal is to help players have the greatest experience possible, so they look back and think, *That was the most fun I've ever had!*

Frankly, that should be your goal as a leader, too (see Chapter 5).

The truth is that twenty-five- and fifty-year-olds have the same desire as ten-year-olds. They want to enjoy the experience, and they don't want to be talked down to, teased, yelled at, or publicly humiliated.

Stop that behavior. It accomplishes nothing, except for making you look like a jerk and making your players want to leave.

We're all human. We think unkind thoughts at times. But not every thought deserves oxygen. Don't judge yourself if you slip up. Simply learn to keep those thoughts to yourself. What comes into your brain doesn't need to come out of your mouth. After all, words last longer than strategy decks. Choose them carefully.

Whether you're leading kids or adults, it's important to gain some self-awareness in this area. Learn to step out of your body and examine your behavior and the impact it has on those around you. Because, whether you realize it or not, your words can leave scars.

I've seen this firsthand watching the coach of a friend's son, "Liam." When Liam was eight, a player made a mistake on the field and the coach slammed a lacrosse stick across the equipment and broke the stick. Because *an eight-year-old* made a mistake. When Liam was thirteen, his team played against that same coach. Afterward, the coach gave Liam a ride home, along with his son and several other players. During the car ride, the coach yelled out "Liam sucks! Liam sucks!" for no apparent reason other than he could. Today, Liam is twenty-four years old and he still remembers the pain caused by this coach.

Coaches like that abuse the power they've been given. They let the title go to their heads.

I've seen this in the workplace, too. "Elsa" ran our CSM team for two years and then asked for the chief customer success title. We gave it to her, and that was the end. She couldn't handle it. The title went straight to her head, and she started crippling people because she was the chief now. She stopped collaborating with her peers and started pulling rank.

Worse, she began acting with misleading intentions. To her team's face, she'd say, "This looks great. You're doing a fantastic job." Then, behind their backs, she'd rip the work apart. I remember one instance where she praised someone in person for an email they'd written, only to email them later and tear the message down and change every detail she'd previously approved. Instead of setting her team up for success, she created confusion, mistrust, and fear.

Once I got wind of what was going on, the castle started crumbling and I knew I had to take action on what we stand for at Dakota. Elsa eventually got removed from the company.

Whether on the field, on the court, or in the office, leading is a bigger responsibility than many people realize. If they truly understood the enormity, they'd be much more mindful about their behavior and words.

SET THE TONE

Everyone wants to be part of a championship culture—kids and adults alike. As a coach/leader, can you help your team do that without being a jerk? Absolutely, but it requires self-awareness and learning from your mistakes like I did. Remember, I'm writing this from a place of compassion. I was the one who asked Chandler a stupid question and erupted into Gui-canoes in the office. You have to be willing to honestly reflect on your own behavior. I don't mean beat yourself up, but do acknowledge where you've abused the title and then move on.

You also set the tone by making the playing experience

fun. Don't treat every game like it's life or death. Instead, teach everyone to play their own game.

When I coached, I often told the kids, "You're a golfer, so you just need to focus on *your* game. You can't control what's happening two fairways over. Let everyone else be. If you focus on your game, everything else will be fine."

That's really the art of life, isn't it? There's so much we can't control. If we watch the news and look at what's going on in our country today, we can lose hope. Don't worry about all that. Focus on your game, on what you can control.

Another way to set the tone is to start with the end in mind. Months before golf season started, I would ask the kids to visualize themselves at the end of the season, walking to the parking lot with their bags on their shoulders after the last match of the year. Then I would ask, "What do you want to have accomplished when the season ends? Do you want to go undefeated in the league? Do you want to win the state championship? Do you want to beat our arch rival in the last match of the year?"

Then I would ask, "If those are your goals, what are you going to do in six months when the season starts to make those goals a reality?"

My goal was to help my players create a vision for themselves, and the team, and then take actions to help them get there—to bring out the best in my players and enable them to become the best versions of themselves.

That should be the goal of every coach and every leader: Set the vision, remove obstructions, and let your team members thrive.

> LEADERSHIP IS LIKE LITTLE LEAGUE: SET HIGH
> STANDARDS, MAKE IT FUN, AND USE YOUR WORDS
> TO BUILD PEOPLE UP, NOT TEAR THEM DOWN.

BE LIKE MR. BERG

One of the greatest coaching moments I ever experienced as a player came from Mr. Berg, the English teacher who treated me like a friend.

When I was a kid, my dad belittled and teased me relentlessly. He didn't celebrate my accomplishments. Nothing I did was ever good enough for him. Just one example: During one hockey game I scored a hat trick (three goals), and my uncles were there to watch. Afterward, we drove from Philly to New York City, where we all gathered at my dad's apartment. My uncles kept talking about the game and the goals I scored. Suddenly, my dad turned to me and said, "Hey, when are we gonna stop talking about your frickin' hat trick?"

My dad also had a short temper and exploded when anything went wrong. His treatment of me was a direct result of the way his father treated him: My grandfather beat him badly more than once. My father never hit me, but his abusive words caused just as much damage.

As a result, I was a very angry person for a very long time. It came out in the way I treated my classmates. We had some Hall of Fame wise asses in my high school class, and of that group, I was voted most sarcastic. Looking back, I'm ashamed at the way I treated people.

My anger also came out on the ice. If someone missed a pass or whiffed on a shot in front of the goal, I'd get in his face on the bench and scream at him. My senior year my temper was particularly bad because we were having a shitty season, my friend and teammate "Bob" was going through public humiliation because of something his dad did, and my parents were getting a divorce.

My coach was so fed up with my attitude that he called Mr. Berg and told him he was thinking of kicking me off the team.

"I don't think that's the right approach with Gui," Mr. Berg said. "Let me talk to him."

So, Mr. Berg called me and said, "I just got off the phone with Coach. He wants to kick you off the team. I told him that's not the best way to deal with you, but I really need you to step up and not be such an agitator."

Before he hung up, Mr. Berg said, "And by the way, you're yelling at everybody else. How about you look at your own stats. You've scored one goal in ten games."

That was a pretty ugly reality check, but Mr. Berg delivered it with kindness.

The next day I called a team meeting, and I told Bob he wasn't invited. "Look," I told the guys, "we need to completely reset and refocus. We need to play for Bob. We need to make this season work."

Then before the game, I sat down with each player individually, no matter if they were playing or sitting on the bench, and I told them how important they were to the team and our success.

We went out and destroyed our opponent. I scored one

goal and had three assists. Afterward, as we were walking out of the locker room, the dean of students came over to me and said, "What in the world was that? You looked like a completely different team!"

Two nights later, I did the same thing: I talked to each player individually before the game, told them how well they were playing, and then we blew out the number one team in the league. I scored three goals and had one assist.

The morning after each of those games, we were still enjoying our victories in homeroom. Mr. Berg walked in after the second game, looked straight at me, and said, "All right. Now I know who to go to when I want to get something done."

That was a defining moment in my life as a leader. It showed me what I'm capable of. Someone believed in me, and I rose to the occasion. To this day I go back to this situation to remind myself that leadership isn't about barking orders or pointing out mistakes. It's about treating people with kindness.

Your players and your team members need a leader like Mr. Berg. Someone who believes in them and treats them with respect. Someone who understands that as a leader, they're playing with fire—that their words can have a lifelong impact, whether positive or negative. When your team knows you believe in them, they will have fun, play with confidence, and accomplish far more than they thought they could.

Two years ago, my son Mac played in the lacrosse Division I Final Four in front of thirty-two thousand people at Lincoln Financial Field. During the warm-up and the pre-game team meeting, the coach created an atmosphere that allowed the players to play relaxed and free. In the end, Mac's team lost on a controversial call in overtime.

Despite that disappointing outcome, however, Mac said to me after the game, "Dad, that game was the most fun I've ever had playing lacrosse." He played at the highest level of collegiate lacrosse *and* he had fun, thanks to the atmosphere created by the coaching staff. That's the spirit of Little League we should take into every organization.

KINDNESS CALL TO ACTION

1. *Don't abuse the title.* Leadership, whether in Little League or the office, doesn't give you permission to blurt out the first thing that comes to mind.
2. *Make it fun.* Your goal isn't to win the World Series of youth sports; it's to create an environment where people love the game and want to come back.
3. *Believe in your team.* Your words can instill confidence that lasts a lifetime, or scars that do the same. Choose carefully.

Conclusion

At the 2016 Live2Lead leadership conference, Simon Sinek told a story about leadership. While staying at the Four Seasons Hotel in Las Vegas, Sinek met a barista named Noah. Noah wasn't just good—he was exceptional. He greeted regulars by name, made great coffee, and brought real enthusiasm to the job.

Simon asked him, "Do you like your job?"

Noah didn't even hesitate. "I love my job."

So Simon pressed further, "What is the Four Seasons doing that makes you feel that way?"

Again, without missing a beat, Noah said, "They care about me. They ask how I'm doing, what I need to do my job better. And it's not just my manager. Any manager here will check in. I feel like I can be myself."

Here's the kicker: Noah also worked at Caesars Palace.

"At Caesars," he said, "the managers are trying to make sure we are doing everything right—they catch us when we do things wrong. I just try to keep my head down and do my job, so I can get my paycheck."

Same person. Same job. A completely different experience. Why? Leadership and culture.

As leaders, it's easy to blame our people. It's harder, but far more honest, to look at the environment we've created. At the Four Seasons, leaders built a culture of trust and care. Noah thrived. At Caesars, they led with fear and control. Noah shut down.

If you want people to love their work, build a place worth loving.

Noah's story isn't unique. People experience negative work cultures in coffee bars, in cubicles, and on Zoom calls every single day. Unfortunately, those environments are not only unenjoyable, but they can also slowly chip away at mental well-being and personal fulfilment.

When people are met with micromanagement like Noah was, or with ridicule and sarcasm, when they're treated like children and prevented from completing projects that provide a sense of accomplishment, that has a negative impact on their overall quality of life. How people are treated at work matters more than most leaders are willing to admit. That environment shapes an individual's confidence, self-worth, and dignity.

At Dakota, I've chosen a different path.

I truly believe, and operate on the principle, that kindness and performance are not mutually exclusive. You can lead with empathy and still win. You can build people up and still hold them accountable. You can care deeply about your team's lives outside of work and still expect them to bring their best selves to the job.

That's why at Dakota, it's not only accepted that people attend a child's recital, show up at their playoff game, or prioritize whatever their family's most important moments may be—it's expected. Family First is one of our mottos. I often joke that you'll be fired if you don't go. But I'm only half joking, because I believe it that strongly.

I've never missed a Penn State lacrosse game for my two sons, and I've loved every second of watching my daughter compete on the squash court. I want my team to know, without a doubt, that it's not only okay to show up for your family; it's essential.

Be Kind is about building better teams. It's about creating a thriving culture. It's about leading with integrity. But more than that, it's about understanding this one powerful truth: How you treat other people at work might be the most important leadership decision you make. And when you build a culture around it, people don't just perform better; they live better.

The bottom line is this: How people are treated at work matters. As we've discussed, conventional wisdom says being a dick is the only way to get results. That's simply not true. You can have both: a culture of kindness in which people feel valued, appreciated, and accomplished *and* an environment where people compete at the highest level. From a mental health perspective, you need to have both.

Your words outlive your title. Choose them as if they'll echo forever—because they will.

CALL TO ACTION

So, how do you make sure the environment you create at work is enjoyable and healthy? Start here.

1. PRACTICE SELF-REFLECTION

Many leaders can't see themselves as they are. They don't have the ability to observe their own behavior and then question that behavior. That's the first place to start if you want to create a culture of kindness.

As we've said throughout the book, your words matter. You don't have to say everything that pops into your head. Learn to observe yourself from the outside and notice when you're being flippant, hostile, and aggressive, when you think you're being funny, but you're actually saying something hurtful. Be hyper-aware of how you speak—almost like your words are coming out in slow motion. Notice not just what you're saying, but also how it lands. Reading the room is a key leadership skill. Look at the expressions on people's faces. See the impact your words have on your team, take responsibility for your part in that reaction, and strive to show up differently.

Sarcasm is the refuge of the weak mind. I understand why people use it—remember, I was voted most sarcastic—but it's really a sign of laziness. It is the easy way out, rather than thinking about what you really mean and how to say it in the clearest, kindest way. Kindness requires discipline: saying what you mean with respect, no ridicule, no passive aggression.

Self-reflection takes courage. Through it, I've seen how

my hockey star locker room attitude carried over into my early years of leadership, and I'm mortified at my own behavior. I've also realized there's a different way. I don't have to stiff arm my way through life. I can choose clarity over sarcasm, and I can bring people up rather than cutting them down.

2. WRITE DOWN YOUR CORE PRINCIPLES

When you know what you stand for and communicate it to your team, you don't have to worry about being vulnerable. You don't have to hide behind control or layers of bureaucracy to police behavior. People know what's expected, and they know there will be consequences if they violate those principles. You're free to treat them like adults.

That said, if you violate one of your core principles, you have to acknowledge it. Or if someone on the team violates one, you need to have a tough conversation. Don't be nice; be kind. Trust doesn't mean avoidance; it means accountability.

I'm not a big fan of creating generic statements. There's nothing interesting about "We value teamwork" or "Be someone who inspires." At Dakota, we created unique, homegrown principles to communicate what we stand for. For example, "We sell apples to apple buyers" means we focus on customers who are interested in what we sell. "Walk the eight feet" means that we tap into the collective knowledge of the group by walking the eight feet from your office to theirs to ask for help. "Don't go cowboy" reminds people to stay in communication—don't go off and do your own thing, again tapping the collective knowledge of the group.

To create your own personalized core principles, start by asking yourself what your company stands for. Come up with one idea. Then dig deeper. Ask yourself *why* you stand for that. Then ask why again. Ask yourself what you do to execute on that value. Peel back the layers to figure out what you really believe and how you live it. When you do, you'll come up with some original words and phrases that represent that first idea. Then start over with a second core principle. And the third. Start with three to five core principles and go from there. The list for us at Dakota is up to twelve and still growing nearly twenty years later.

Writing down your core principles isn't about controlling people. It's about giving them a framework for success. You are removing confusion, eliminating second-guessing, and showing respect for their ability to rise to the standards.

3. BRING POSITIVE ENERGY

As a leader, your energy is contagious. People feel it the moment you walk into a room. The question is: Do you bring positive energy, or do you bring volatility that makes people walk on eggshells?

We said this back in Chapter 5, and it bears repeating: Your job description as the leader is to make people feel better about themselves when you walk into the room. Not worse.

Your people shouldn't spend their days bracing for mood swings or outbursts. They should know what to expect.

Steady, positive energy creates an environment where people can focus, contribute, and thrive. Volatility does the opposite.

So don't create an atmosphere of fear, hesitation, and silence. No one does their best work here. Instead, treat each person with warmth and respect, the way you would treat a good friend's adult children.

4. GIVE YOURSELF FREEDOM

Leadership is demanding. You carry the weight of accountability, of setting the tone, of building trust. As a leader, you also need to give yourself a sense of freedom.

Freedom doesn't mean doing whatever you want. In this sense, I'm saying free yourself from the need to be "nice," from the fear of discomfort, and from the belief that kindness equals softness. Kindness sometimes requires hard things: acknowledging the elephant in the room, holding the line when it would be easier to avoid it.

And that leads to the ultimate principle: kindness over everything else. Kindness doesn't mean lowering the bar. It means setting the highest standards, enforcing them with compassion, and refusing to tolerate corrosive behavior.

This is my counterpoint to the first three action items. Self-reflection, core principles, and positive energy are all about discipline. Freedom is what balances them. It's what ensures reflection doesn't become self-censorship, principles don't turn into bureaucracy, and positive energy doesn't slip into fake cheerleading. This freedom gives you permission to do the hard things, like making sure people know what good looks like, even when that means uncomfortable conversations. You have to acknowledge the elephant in the room. You have to be kind and not worry about being nice.

In leading from this place, you give yourself the freedom to be both kind and strong, and that's the kind of leadership people will follow.

NO DOWNSIDE

Chances are you're in a leadership position because you see something different in the business or organization, or perhaps you bring different experience—you're seeing something others don't. And when you see something different, you might not have the patience to bring people along.

As a result, you can become very judgmental. You might think, "Come on, are you an idiot? You don't get it?"

In this mindset, some leaders use their unique insight or experience as a beat down to tease others. That kind of behavior is never appropriate, but especially when the only reason they have the upper hand is years of learning. People need a safe environment in which to gain that same insight. They actually want to learn and grow. As a leader, having compassion and thoughtfulness moves mountains. Without it, people will leave and the organization will suffer as a result.

There are tens of thousands of books on leadership. This is simply my story and the lessons I've learned. I'm not perfect, and I don't have all the answers. But I have seen the power of this radically different approach. There is no downside. You're not giving up anything when you treat others with respect. Instead, you're creating an environment in which people become the best versions of themselves and perform at the highest level.

Be clear. Be kind. Lead in a way that makes people not only work better, but live better.

Who wouldn't want to be part of that?

Acknowledgments

Leadership is hard. This book is a collection of lessons learned from my own personal journey—one that is ongoing and far from perfect. I have made many mistakes along the way, but my goal has always been, and will always remain, to create a great place to work by being thoughtful with my words and how I treat people.

I want to thank my wife, Susan, and my three children, Mac, Cate, and Will, for their excitement, encouragement, and unwavering support.

To my parents, Judy and Jerry Kling: Thank you for showing me a lifetime of kindness and unconditional support. Your example has been an extraordinary gift.

I am also deeply grateful to Alan Breed and the team at Edgewood, and to Mark Stitzer and the team at Hamlin. Without their belief in me and their support, I would not have the career I do today.

To the entire Dakota team: Thank you for living the

principles of kindness every day—not because anyone asked you to, but because of the kind of people you are. You embody these values naturally, and that is what makes Dakota such a special place.

My heartfelt thanks to Gail Fay, my ghostwriter, whose craft and steady partnership brought clarity, momentum, and polish to these ideas. And to Morgan Holycross, my co-author, for your insight, rigor, and voice—you strengthened this book at every turn.

Finally, to Mr. Berg—Barry Berg—who, with one phone call in January of 1985, changed the course of my life and showed me what I was capable of.

About the Author

GUI COSTIN is the founder and CEO of Dakota, a financial software, data, and media company based in Philadelphia. Dakota's core platform, Dakota Marketplace, is a database of LPs, GPs, private companies, and public companies that helps fundraising and deal-sourcing teams raise capital and identify investment opportunities. Today, more than 1,300 investment firms rely on Dakota to power their workflows. Gui lives in Bryn Mawr, Pennsylvania, with his family and two dogs.

MORGAN HOLYCROSS is a marketing manager at Dakota, leading content and product marketing and supporting investment events in the US and Europe.